INDIA.ARIE

Testimony: vol. 1, Life & Relationship

T0040772

Art Direction/Design by: Annalee Valencia-Bruch
Photography by: Jimmy Bruch

CONTENTS

INTRO: LOVING

Words and Music by
INDIA.ARIE

love with an o - pen heart,___ to love with an o - pen heart,___ to

love with an o - pen heart._____ I wan-na love___ with an o-pen heart.___

Oh,___ ooh,_____ with an

o - pen heart.___

THESE EYES

Words and Music by
INDIA.ARIE, JOYCE SIMPSON
and MARK BATSON

Verse 2:
All this cryin', all this fightin' simply ain't my style,
Though you're one of the most important people in my life.
I loved you from the day we met, I know you loved me too.
But at this point, walking away is the best thing we can do.
(To Chorus:)

Verse 3:
Were we meant to be man and wife?
The answer, I don't know.
Of life's many mysteries, what intrigues me the most
Is who our children would have been.
I guess we'll never know.
Even as I walk away, I'll always keep the hope.
(To Chorus:)

THE HEART OF THE MATTER

Words and Music by
DON HENLEY, MIKE CAMPBELL
and JOHN DAVID SOUTHER

Moderately ♩ = 96

(with pedal)

Verse:

1. I got the call to-day, I did-n't wan-na hear, but I
2. *See additional lyrics*

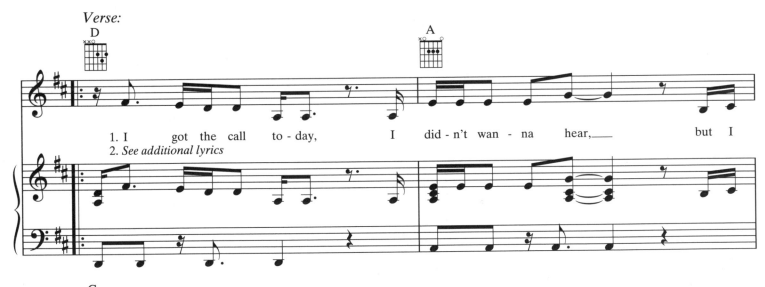

knew that it would come.

The Heart of the Matter - 7 - 1
26281

An old,____ true friend of ours was talk - in' on____ the phone.____ She said you'd

found____ some - one._____ And I

thought of all____ the bad____ luck, and all the strug-gles we____ went through,____ how

I lost me,____ and you lost you.____ What were all these voic - es out-

20

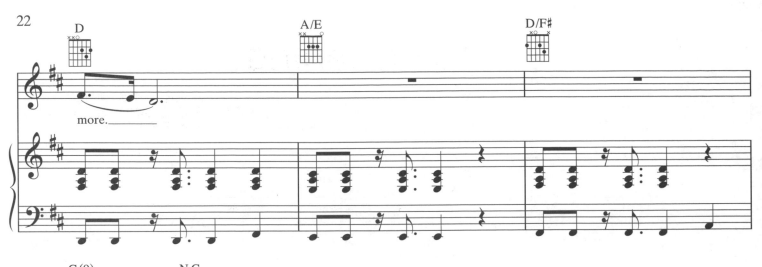

Repeat ad lib. and fade

Verse 2:
These times are so uncertain,
There's a yearning undefined,
And people filled with rage.
We all need a little tenderness.
How can love survive in such a graceless age?
And the trust and self-assurance
That lead to happiness
Are the very things we kill, I guess.
Pride and competition cannot fill these empty arms,
And the wall they put between us,
You know it doesn't keep us warm.

Chorus 2:
I've been tryin' to live without you now,
But I miss you, baby.
And the more I know, the less I understand.
All the things I thought I'd figured out,
I had to learn again.
I've been trying to get down
To the heart of the matter,
But my will gets weak,
And my heart is so shattered,
But I think it's about forgiveness, forgiveness,
Even if, even if you don't love me anymore.
(To Bridge:)

Chorus: (On D.S.):
I've been tryin' to get down
To the heart of the matter,
Because the flesh gets weak,
And the ashes will scatter.
So, I'm thinkin' about
Forgiveness, forgiveness,
Even if you don't love me anymore.
Even if you don't love me anymore.

GOOD MOURNING

Words and Music by
INDIA.ARIE, SHANNON SANDERS
and DREW RAMSEY

Verses 2 & 3:

Good mourn-ing to the pain in the cen-ter of my chest._____

It's cra-zy how much___ I___ miss_____

a sim-ple good-morn—ing kiss,___ oh._____

2. Good mourn-ing, in-to
3. Good mourn-ing to

de - pen - dence, or is it lone - li - ness?_____
the harsh re - al - i - ties of life._____

4. Good mourn-ing, ac - cep-tance, good mourn-ing, in - ner strength._____

I know that God's will will be done, so, it's a good mourn-ing af - ter all.

Freely

PRIVATE PARTY

Words and Music by
INDIA.ARIE, BRANDEN BURCH,
RICHARD JOHNSON JR. and JOHN HOWARD

Verse 2:

2. I'm gon - na take__ off all my clothes, look at my - self__ in the mir - ror.

We're gon - na have__ a con - ver - sa - tion, we're gon - na heal__ the dis - con - nec - tion.

I don't re - mem - ber when it start - ed, but this is where it's gon - na end.__

My bod - y is beau - ti - ful and sa - cred and I'm gon - na cel - e - brate_____

Chorus:

_ it.   I'm hav-ing a pri - vate par - ty.   Ain't no-bod-y here_ but

me and my an - gels and my_ gui-tar sing-in', "Ba - by, look_ how far_   we've come,

yeah."   I'm hav-in' a pri - vate par - ty,   learn - ing how_ to love_

_ me,_   cel - e-brat - ing   the wom-an I've_ be-come,_   yeah.

Bridge:

All my life, I've been look-ing for some-bod-y else to make me whole. But I had to learn the hard way true love be-gins with me. This is not e-go or van-i-ty, I'm just cel-e-brat-ing me.

Chorus:

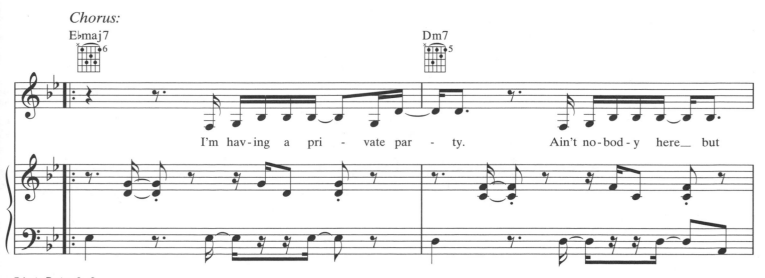

Verse 3:
Sometimes I'm alone but never lonely,
That's what I've come to realize.
I've learned to love the quiet moments,
The Sunday mornings of life,
Where I can reach deep down inside,
Or out into the universe.
I can laugh until I cry,
Or I can cry away the hurt.
(To Chorus:)

THERE'S HOPE

Words and Music by
INDIA.ARIE, BRANDEN BURCH
and ANTHONY HARRINGTON

Moderate R & B feel ♩ = 88

(Play 8vb lower throughout)

Verse:

1. Back when I had a lit - tle,___ I thought that I need-ed a lot.___ A
2. *See additional lyrics*

There's Hope - 7 - 1
26281

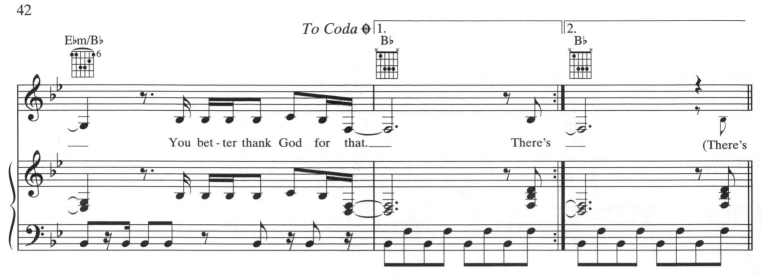

Bridge:

But we got-ta keep on sur-viv-ing, keep liv-ing our truth and do the best we can do___ 'cause there's

Coda

Vocal break:

There's hope. Stand up for your rights, keep shin-ing your

light, and show the world your smile.___ Stand up for your

rights, keep shin-ing your light, and show the world your smile.___ There's

Chorus:

Outro:

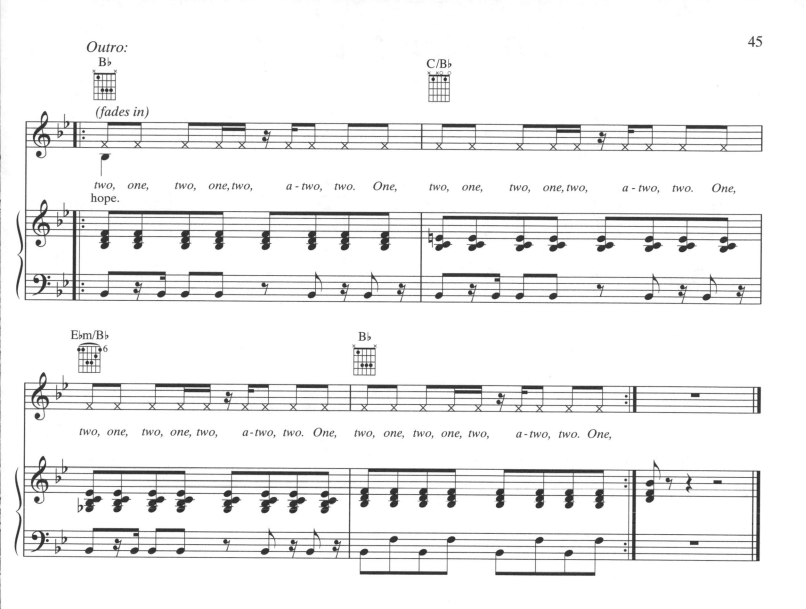

Verse 2:
(There's hope.)
Off in the backcountry of Brazil,
I met a young brotha that made me feel
That I could accomplish anything.
You see, just like me he wanted to sing.
He had no windows and no doors.
He lived a simple life and was extremely poor.
On top of all of that he had no eyesight,
But that didn't keep him from seein' the light.
He said, "What's it like in the U.S.A.?"
And all I did was complain.
He said, "Living here is paradise."
He taught me paradise is in your mind.
You know that…
(To Chorus:)

INTERLUDE: LIVING

Words and Music by
INDIA.ARIE

INDIA'S SONG

Words and Music by
INDIA.ARIE

Rubato

Moderately ♩ = 92

Verses 1 & 2:

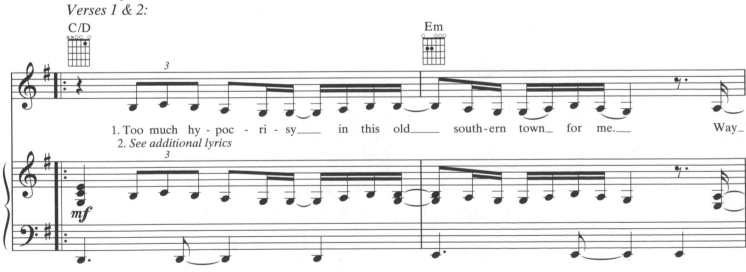

1. Too much hy-poc-ri-sy___ in this old___ south-ern town_ for me.___ Way

2. *See additional lyrics*

India's Song - 7 - 1
26281

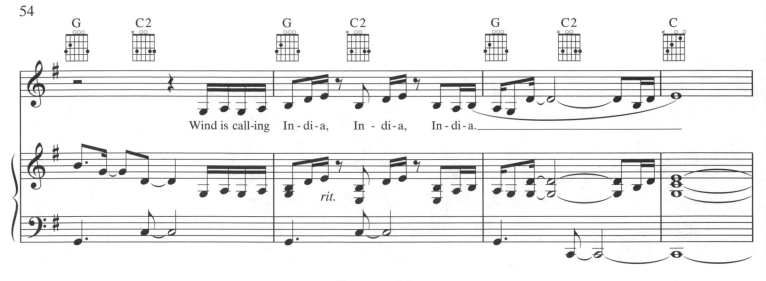

Wind is call-ing In - di - a, In - di - a, In - di - a.____

Slower, with movement

Instrumental:

N.C.

(with vocal ad libs.)

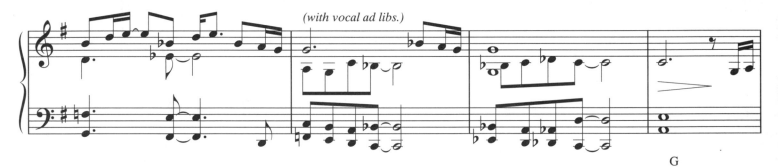

Verse 2:
It's the typical savannah day,
So I take my guitar to the park and I play.
Sitting up under the live oak trees,
The strangest feeling came over me.
Is this the tree where my brother was hung?
Is this the ground where his body was burned?
God gave to me the gift of song,
So I dedicate this one.
(To Chorus:)

WINGS OF FORGIVENESS

Words and Music by
INDIA.ARIE, PHILLIP WHITE
and FRANK MACEK

Moderate hip-hop groove ♩ = 100

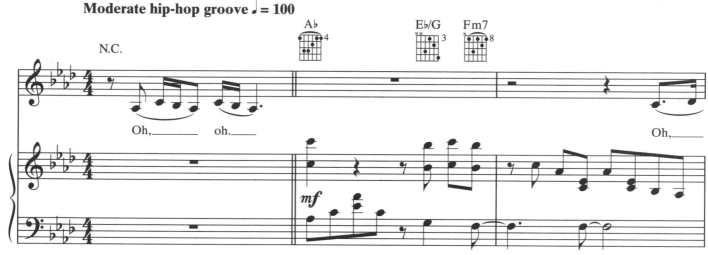

Oh,___ oh.___ Oh,___

___ oh.___ I just want you to

know af-ter ev-'ry-thing that we've been through,___ I just want you to know that I still love___ you,___

Wings of Forgiveness - 8 - 1
26281

Ab   Eb/G   Fm

want to let you know I for-give___ you. I want to let you know I still love___ you.___

Db   Eb

Repeat ad lib. and fade

Want you to know I still love___ you.   I just want you to

Verse 2:
Had to run to the arms of curiosity
Just to find what was here in my life all along.
I have found that the utter simplicity
Simply means making peace with your complexity.
If Gandhi can forgive persecution,
Surely you can forgive me for being so petty.
(To Chorus 2:)

Verse 3:
I took a swim in the sea of guilt and misery
To find myself on an island in the middle of nowhere.
In my solitude I asked in all the highest truth,
And what I was told was to thine own self be true.
If Jesus can forgive crucifixion,
Surely we can survive and find a resolution.
(To Chorus 3:)

SUMMER

Words and Music by
INDIA.ARIE, CINDY MORGAN
and ANDREW RAMSEY

Bridge:

68

Verse 4:

Hel - lo,___ sum - mer,___ a kiss from my___ old friend.___

Been___ such a long___ time,___

tell me how___ you've been?_____ So_____

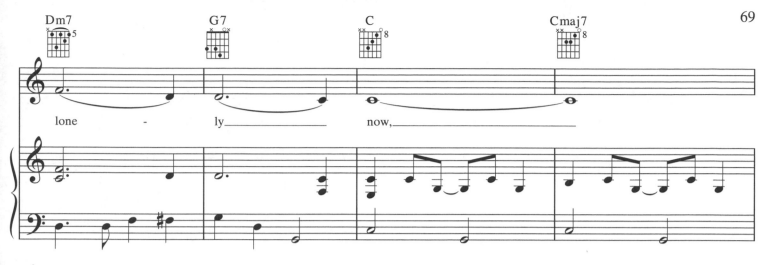

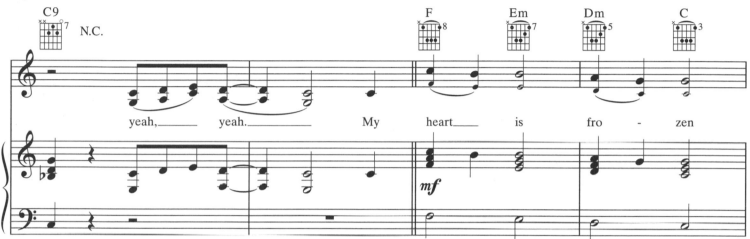

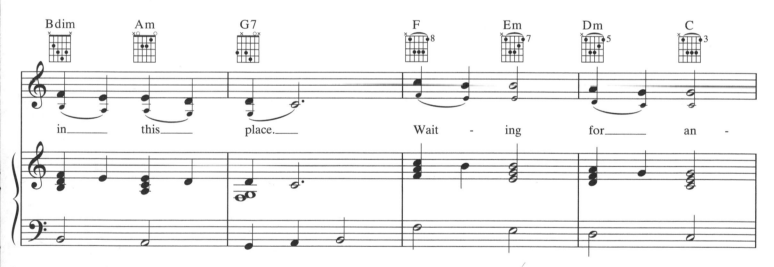

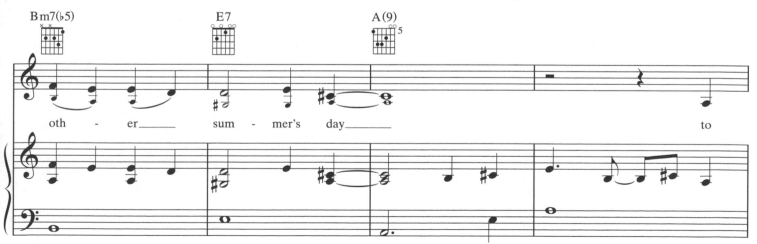

70

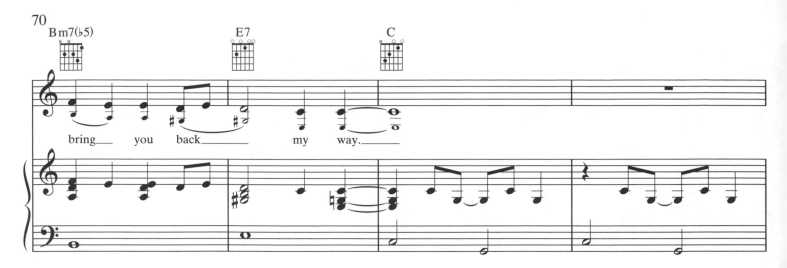

bring___ you back_____ my way.____

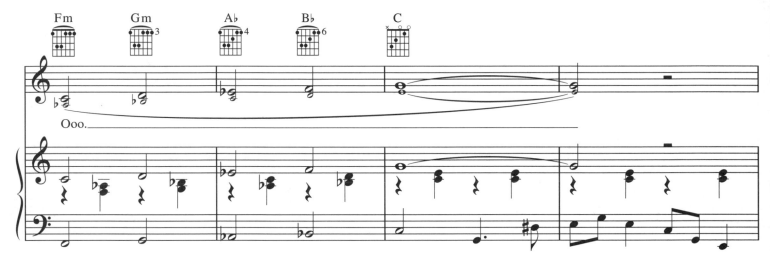

Ooo._____

Ooo._____ Good - bye, sum - mer,___ I

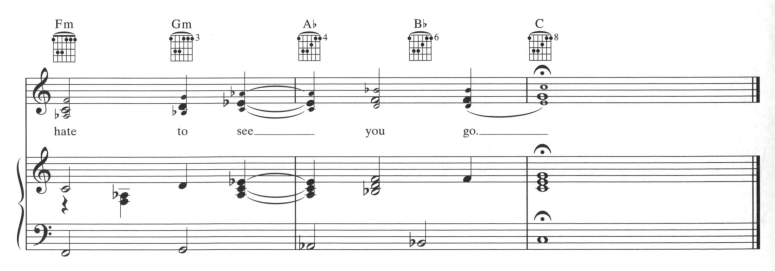

hate to see_____ you go._____

Summer - 8 - 8
26281

I AM NOT MY HAIR

Words and Music by
INDIA.ARIE, SHANNON SANDERS
and ANDREW RAMSEY

shave it off like a South Af - ri - can beau - ty, or get it on lock like Bob Mar - ley.

You can rock it straight like O - prah Win - frey, if it's not what's on your head, it's what's un - der - neath_ and say...

Chorus:

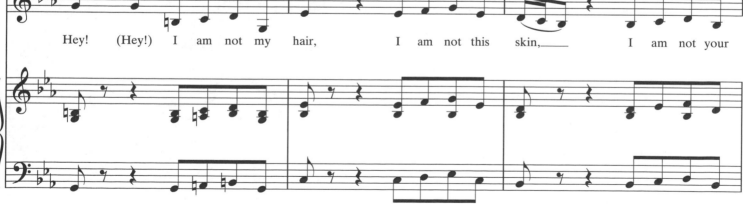

Hey! (Hey!) I am not my hair, I am not this skin,____ I am not your

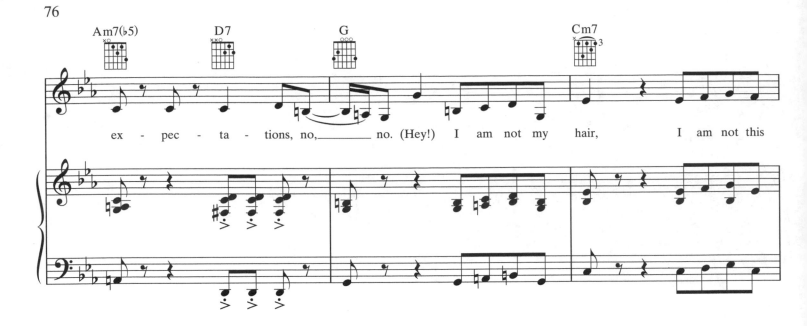

ex - pec - ta - tions, no,_____ no. (Hey!) I am not my hair, I am not this

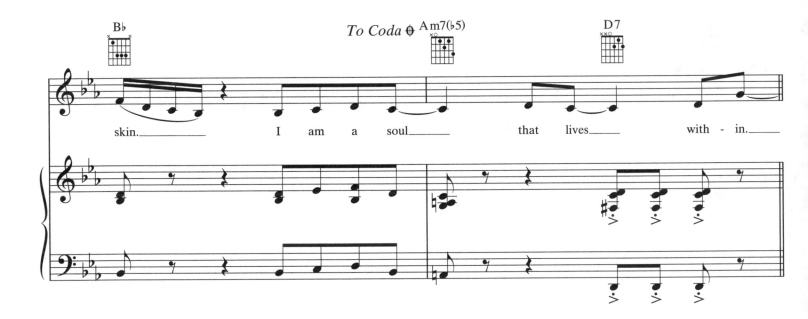

skin._____ I am a soul_____ that lives_____ with - in._____

Bridge:

___ Does the way I wear my hair make me a bet - ter per -

son? Does the way I wear my hair make me a bet - ter friend?

Oh._____ Does the way I wear my hair de - ter - mine my in - teg - ri - ty?____

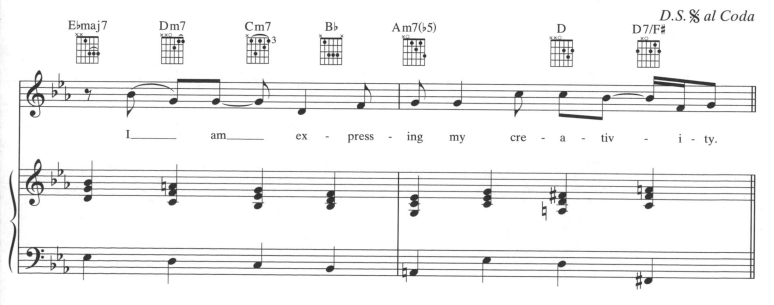

D.S. %al Coda

I____ am____ ex - press - ing my cre - a - tiv - i - ty.

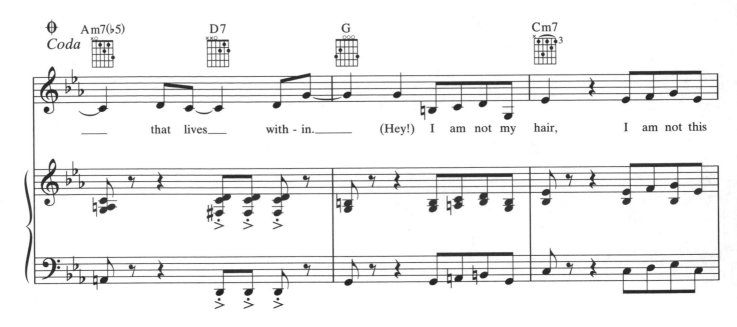

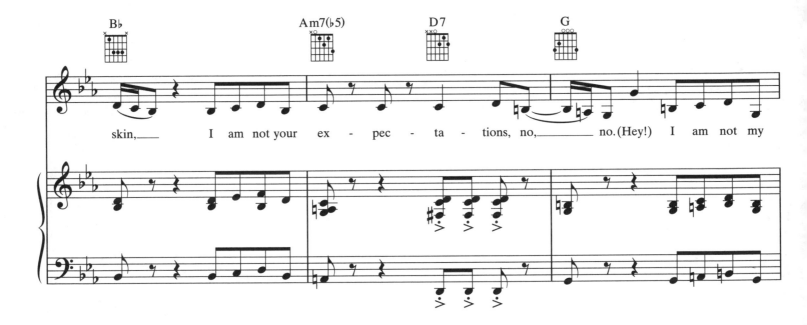

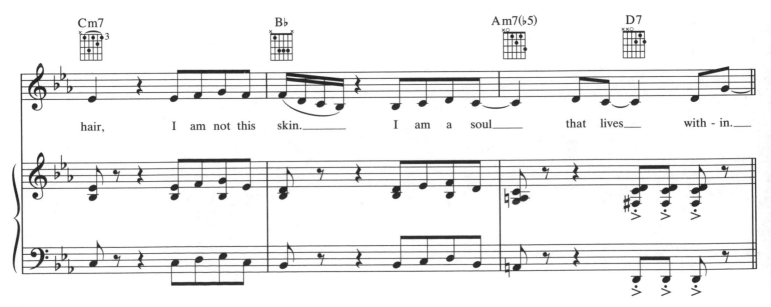

Da da da da___ da da da da.
Da da da da___

Repeat ad lib. and fade

Da da da da___ da da da da.
da da da da. Da da da da___ da da da da.

Verse 3:
Breast cancer and chemotherapy
Took away her crown and glory.
She promised God if she was to survive,
She would enjoy every day of her life.
On national television,
Her diamond eyes are sparkling,
Bald-headed like a full moon shining,
Singing out to the whole wide world like...
(To Chorus:)

BETTER PEOPLE

Words and Music by
INDIA.ARIE, SHANNON SANDERS
and DREW RAMSEY

82

Coda Chorus:

If black_____ peo - ple____

____ would talk to white_____ peo - ple, it would make us a

bet - ter peo - ple_____ all a - round,____ yeah,_____ yeah.__ If Re-

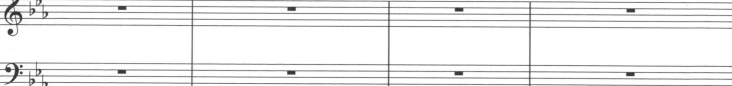

pub - li - can peo - ple_____ would talk to Dem - o - crat - ic___ peo - ple,____ it would make us dip - lo -

mat - ic___ peo - ple_____ all a - round._____

E♭5 E♭/G A♭2   E♭5 E♭/G A♭2

E♭5 E♭/G A♭2   A♭5 B♭5 E♭5

Repeat ad lib. and fade

Verse 2:
We went from radio to TV;
Now we're going from LP to CD.
Don't be afraid to try something new.
I can help you with the brand-new technology.
Help me with the age-old philosophy.
Together there's so much we can do with...
(To Chorus:)

OUTRO: LEARNING

Words and Music by
INDIA.ARIE

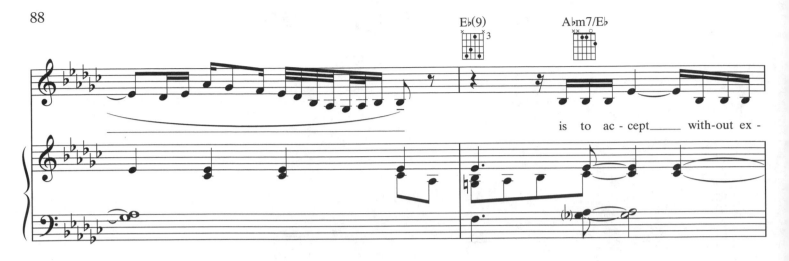

is to ac - cept_____ with-out ex -

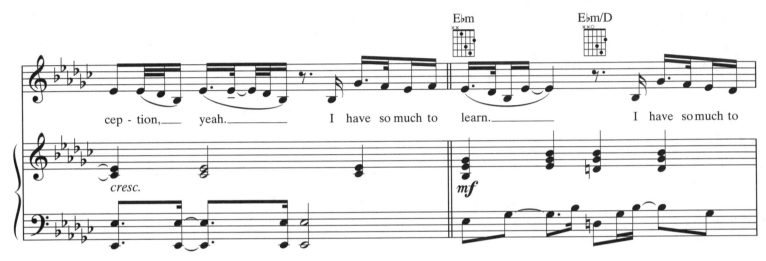

cep - tion,_____ yeah._____ I have so much to learn._____ I have so much to

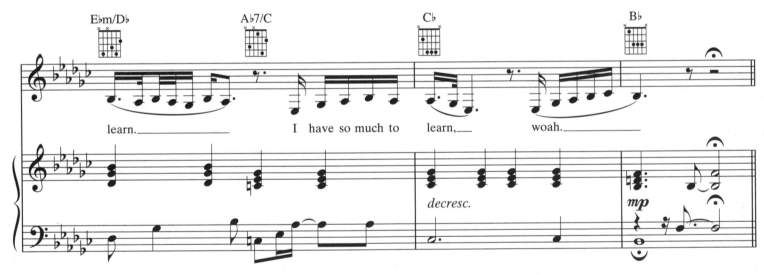

learn._____ I have so much to learn,_____ woah._____

Repeat and fade

a tempo

I CHOOSE

Words and Music by
INDIA.ARIE, ANDREW CASTRO
and MARK BATSON

I Choose - 8 - 1
26281

Bm N.C.

this day for-ward, ev - 'ry de - ci - sion that I make will be my own.__ And I

Chorus:

E7

A7sus

choose to be the best that I can be. I

N.C.

choose {to be cou - ra - geous in / to be au - then - tic in} ev - er - y - thing I

E7

A7sus

do.__ My past__ don't__ dic - tate who I

Release the guilt a-bout why things hap-pen the way they do 'cause life is gon-na do what it do.____ And ev-'ry

Repeat and fade

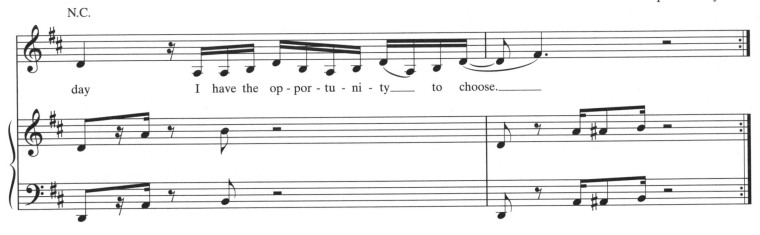

day   I have the op-por-tu-ni-ty____ to choose.____

Verse 2:
I don' been through some painful things
I thought I would never make it through.
Filled up with shame from the top of my head
To the soles of my shoes.
I've put myself in so may chaotic circumstances.
By the grace of God, I've been given so may second chances.

But today I decided to let it all go.
I'm dropping these bags, I'm making room for my joy.
(To Chorus:)

THIS TOO SHALL PASS

Words and Music by
INDIA.ARIE, ANDREW CASTRO
and MARK BATSON

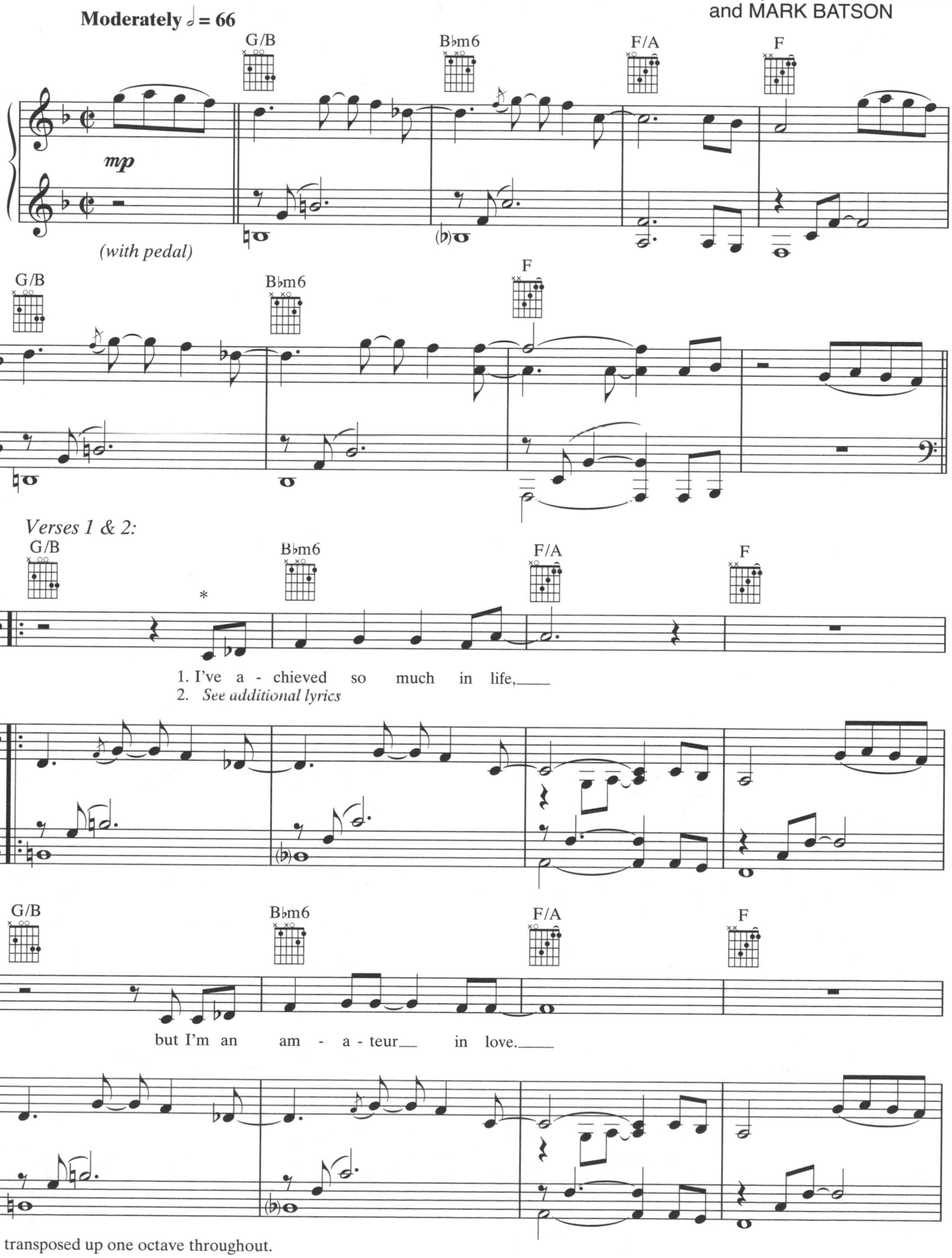

Moderately 𝅗𝅥 = 66
G/B
B♭m6
F/A
F
mp
(with pedal)
G/B
B♭m6
F
Verses 1 & 2:
G/B
B♭m6
F/A
F
*
1. I've a - chieved so much in life,
2. See additional lyrics
G/B
B♭m6
F/A
F
but I'm an am - a - teur in love.

* Vocal transposed up one octave throughout.

My bank ac-count is do-ing just fine,

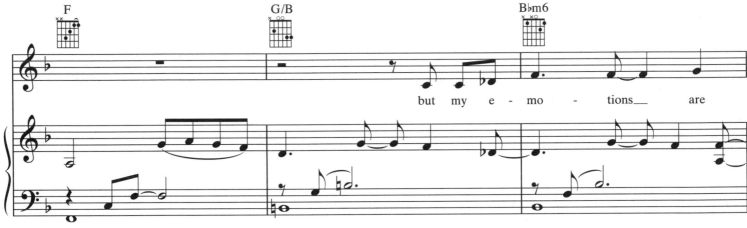

but my e-mo - tions___ are

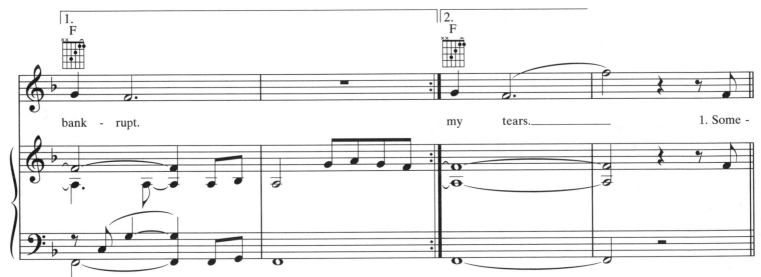

1.
bank - rupt.

2.
my tears._____ 1. Some -

Bridge:

times the pain___ is so___ loud in my heart___ that

when I pray___ for heal - ing in my heart.___ To

This Too Shall Pass - 8 - 2
26281

Coda

Verse 5:

5. All of a sud-den I re - al - ize____ that it on - ly hurts worse to fight_____ it.____ So I em-brace__ my shad - ow,_____ and hold_

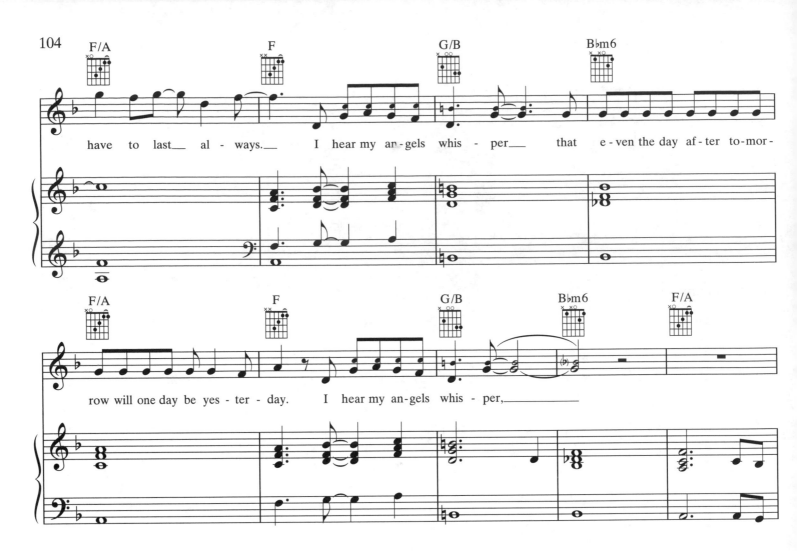

have to last__ al - ways.__ I hear my an-gels whis - per__ that e - ven the day af - ter to-mor-

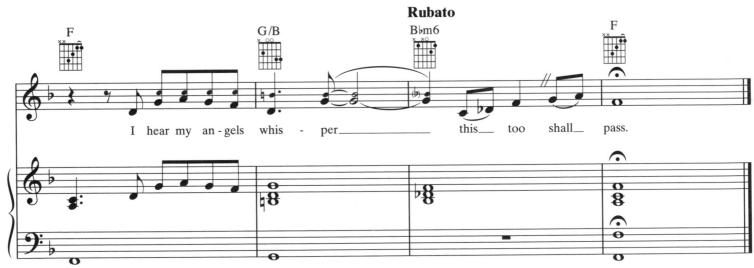

row will one day be yes - ter - day. I hear my an-gels whis - per,_____

Rubato

I hear my an-gels whis - per_____ this__ too shall__ pass.

Verse 2:
My body is nice and strong,
But my heart is in a million pieces.
When the sun is shining, so am I,
But when the night falls, so do my tears.
(To Bridge:)

Verse 4:
My head and my heart are at war,
'Cause love is happening the way I want it.
Feel like I am about to breakdown,
Can't hear the light at the end of the tunnel.
(To Bridge:)